PICTURE ME

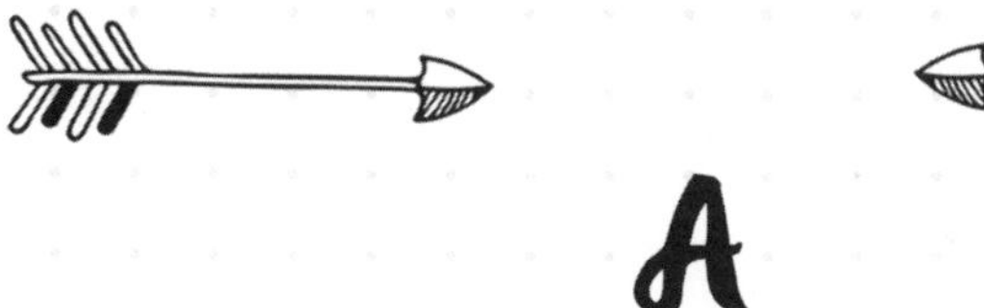

A JOURNAL TO GET LIFE SORTED

Buster Books

Illustrated by Cindy Wilde

Edited by Imogen Williams
Designed by Derrian Bradder,
Zoe Bradley and Jack Clucas
Cover design by Angie Allison

This book was first published in Great Britain in 2018 by Buster Books, an imprint of Michael O'Mara Books Limited,
9 Lion Yard, Tremadoc Road, London SW4 7NQ

 www.busterbooks.co.uk  Buster Children's Books  @BusterBooks

With some material adapted from www.shutterstock.com

ISBN: 978-1-78055-533-1

2 4 6 8 10 9 7 5 3 1

This book was printed in February 2018 by Shenzhen Wing King Tong Paper Products Co. Ltd.,
Shenzhen, Guangdong, China

This journal belongs to

Contents

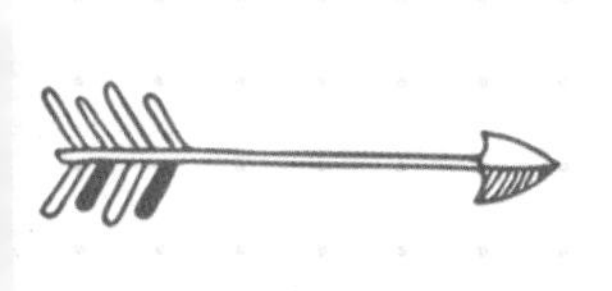

How to use this journal

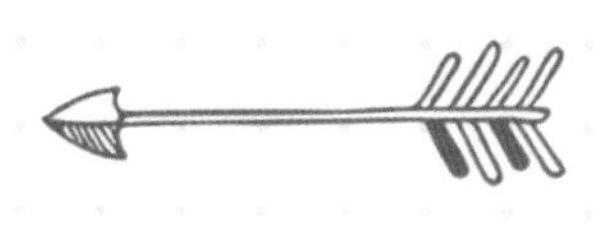

This is your journal to fill in, decorate and design.

Complete each section to help you keep track of things and get organized. There is space for you to jot down life goals and wishlists, as well as record positive thoughts, gift ideas and music playlists.

Use the monthly planners to make a note of all the things you need to do, from meeting friends to completing tasks, and fill in the monthly mood charts to see your emotions in colour.

Don't forget to personalize your journal by adding decorative doodles and symbols to bring each page to life. Turn the page for more ways to use this journal.

Get organizing!

Use these pages to jot down all your plans and tasks for each month to keep track of your deadlines.

Personalize

Be inspired by the 'decorate & design' pages. Add your own doodles and pictures to make this journal truly unique.

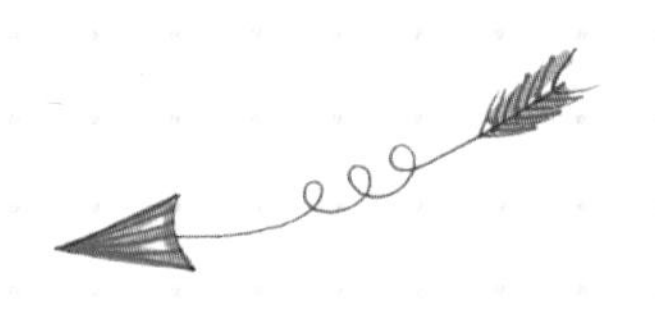

Checklist

There are checklist pages at the back of the book that are completely blank. Personalize them to suit your own life plans. Add decorative borders and use colourful pens to bring these pages to life.

Decorative
inspiration

Decorate & design

Add banners and doodles to pages throughout the book to personalize this journal and make it your own.

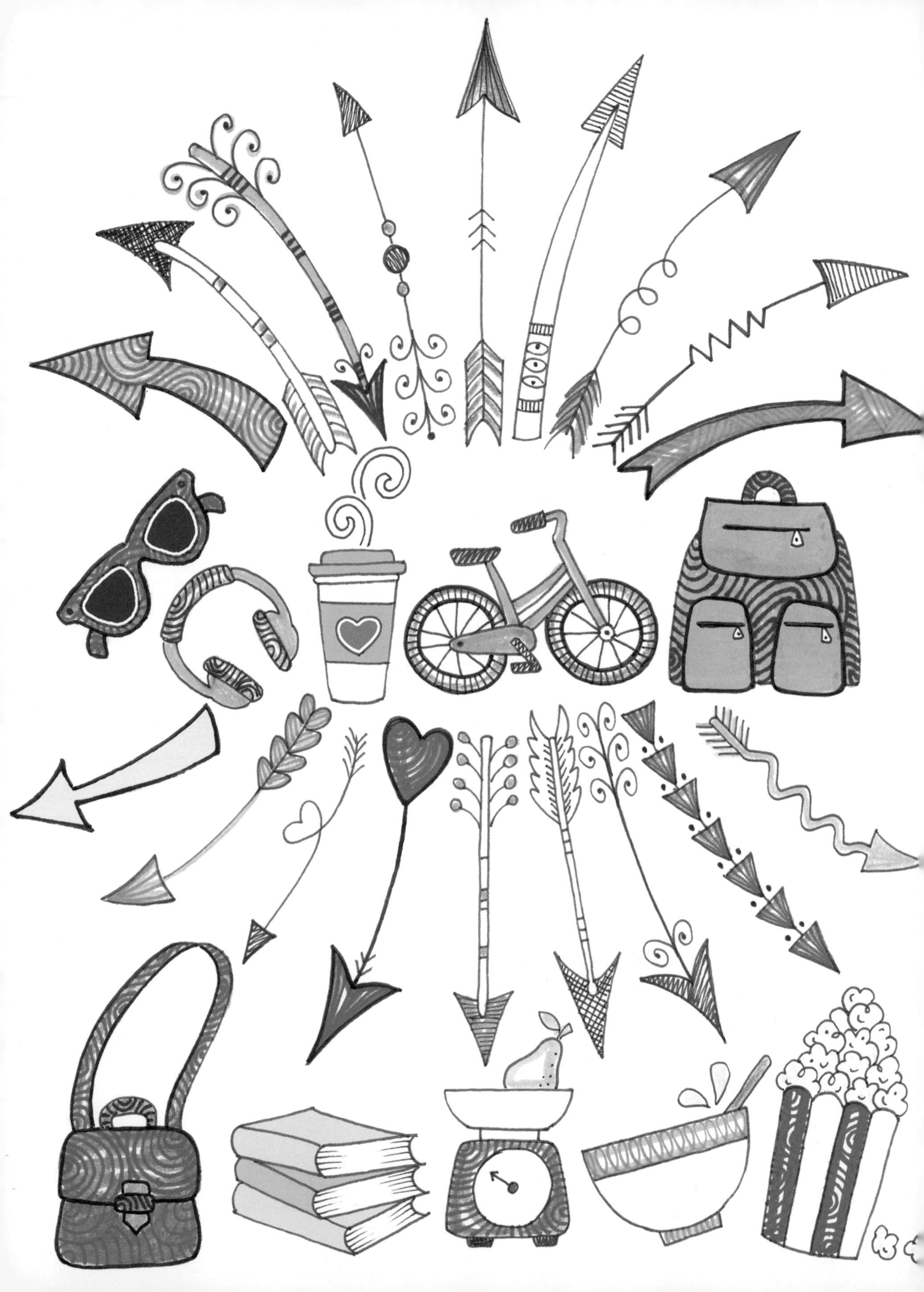

all
about
me

Lights, camera, action

What would the film of your life be called? Brainstorm some ideas and write them in the clapperboards below.

Superstar

Think of five talents you have
and write them inside the stars.

What will be ...

Dream big and let yourself be inspired.
You can look back on this page in years to come.

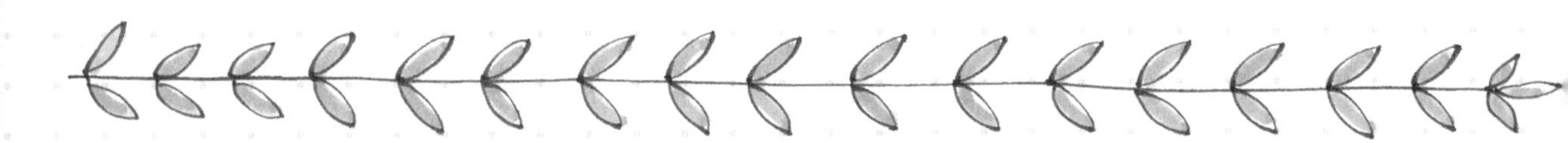

 I am ...

 I have ...

I want to ...

 I will ...

 I love ...

I dream ...

I wish ...

I can ...

I do ...

I make ...

Dream journal

Keep note of your dreams and sleep patterns
to track your sleeping habits.

Fact file

Fill the page with facts all about you. Keep adding to it over time to create a collection of memories.

Life
goals and
wishlists

Send your wishes soaring

Write a wish in every balloon. If it comes true, colour the balloon in. Are there any wishes you could help come true yourself?

Books to read

Fill your bookshelf with all the books you'd like to read. Colour in each one once you've finished it.

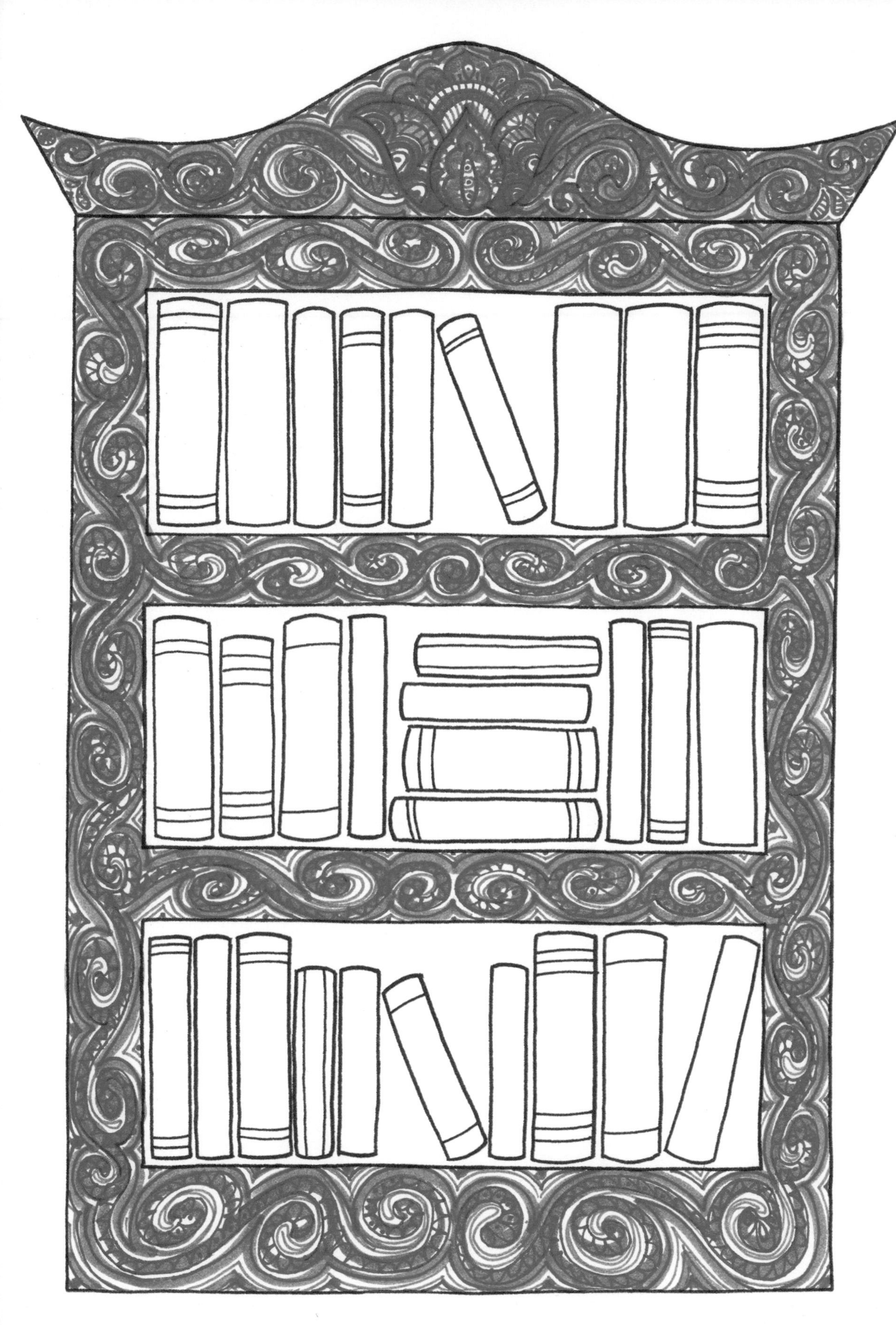

Overcoming fears

Jot down all the fears you want to overcome.
Use banners and doodles to decorate the page.

Tiny adventures

Write a little adventure you'd like to achieve in each segment of the balloon. Colour it in once you've completed the adventure.

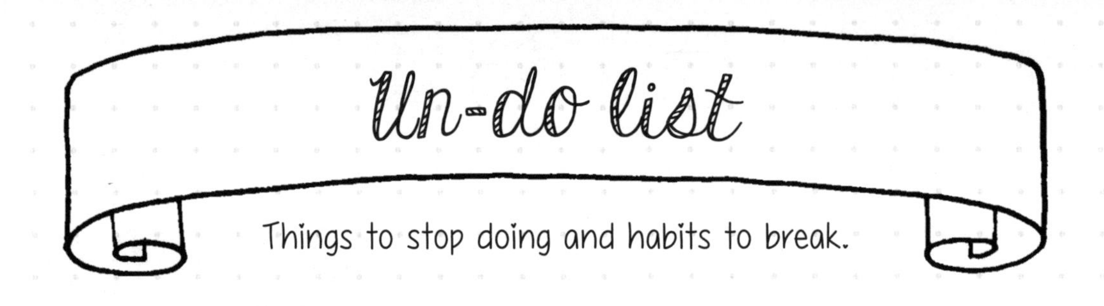
Un-do list
Things to stop doing and habits to break.

Dream jobs

Fill this page with all the jobs you might want to try in the future.

Movies to watch

Fill your film reel with all the movies you'd like to watch. Colour in each square when you've watched it.

Bucket list

Fill the buckets with things you would love to do at some point in your life.

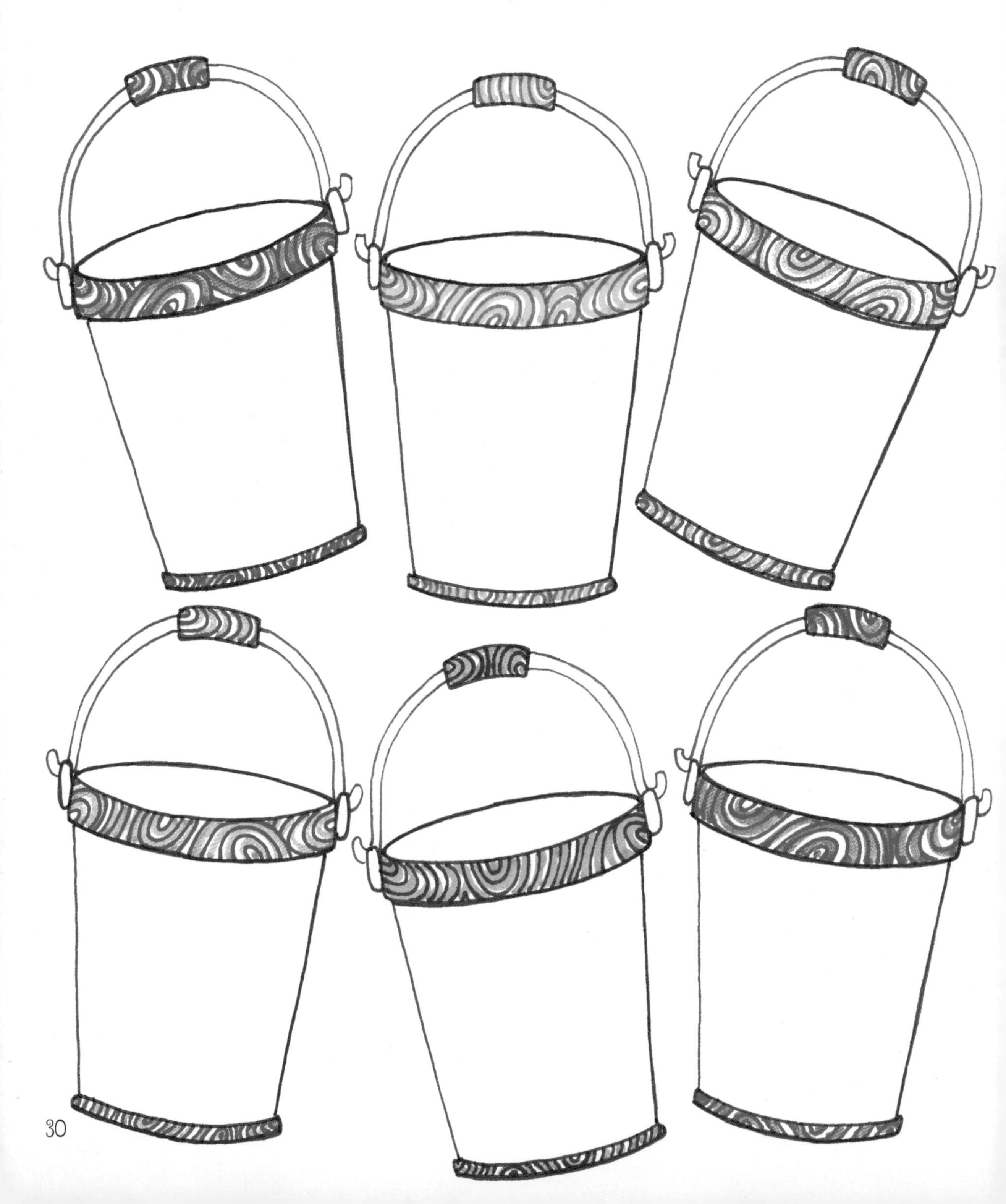

Over the rainbow
Write your best qualities in the rainbow rays.

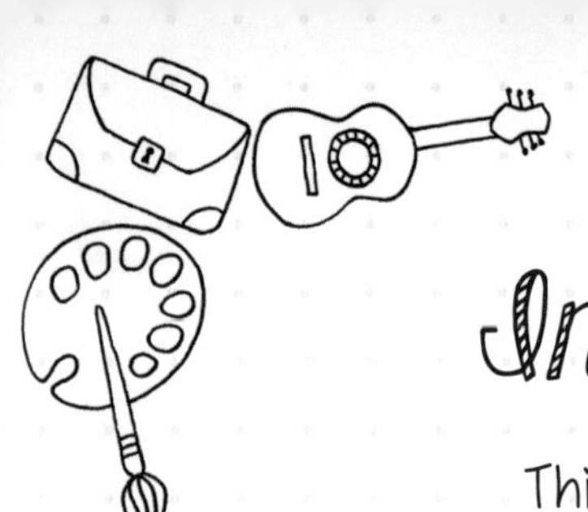

Inspirational people

Think of all the people who inspire you and why.

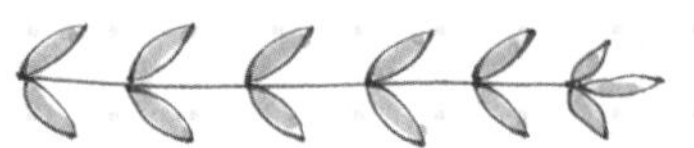

Need to watch

Write down all the shows you want to watch in the televisions below. Colour in each television when you have watched them.

Be

creative

Stories to tell

Fill these pages with ideas for books
or stories that you would like to write.

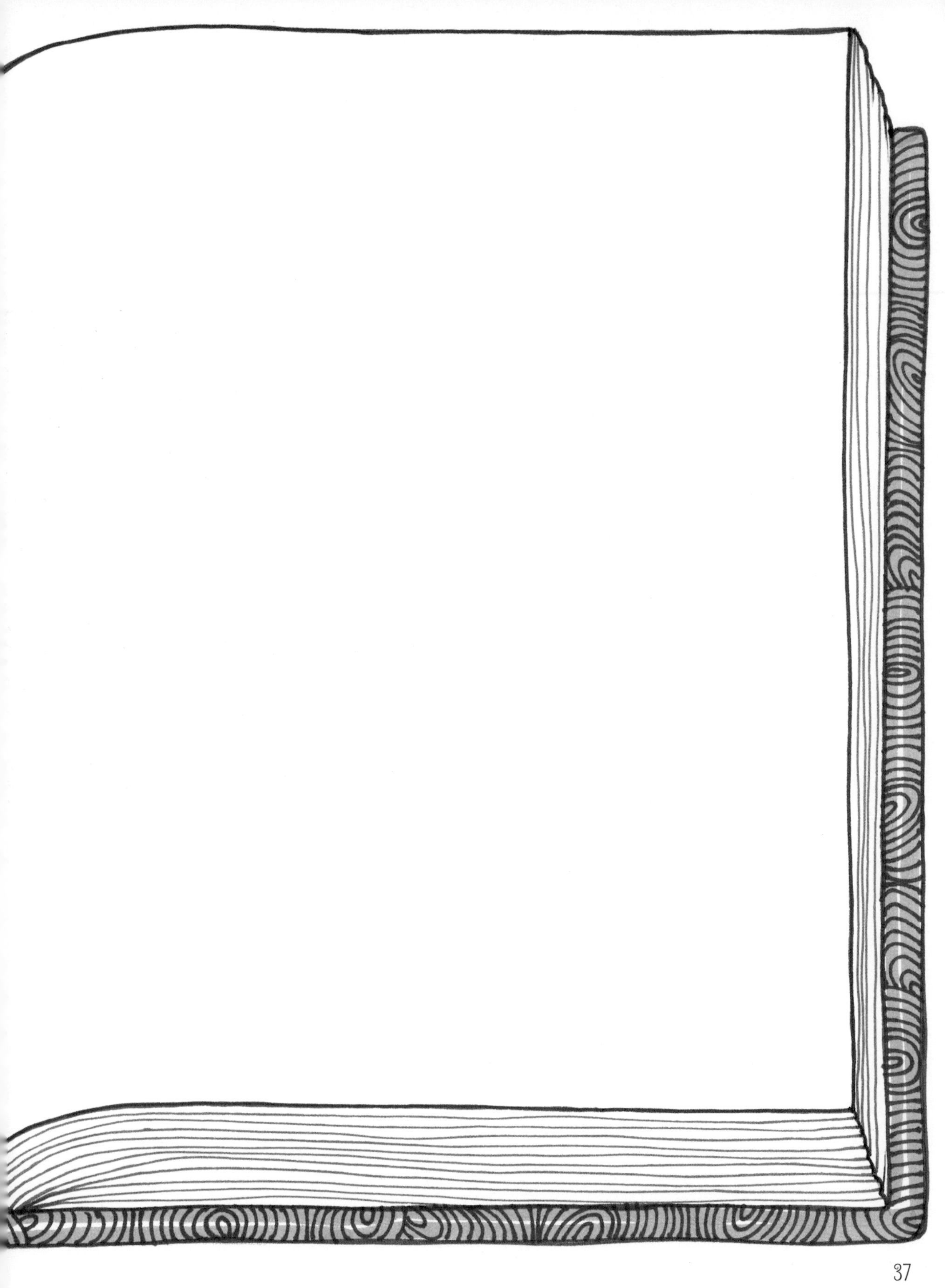

Arts & crafts

Get creative and fill the easel with craft projects to try.

Doodlebomb

Doodle all over this page to
de-stress and release your creative energy.

Recipe ideas

Use the mixing bowls to record recipes that you want to try. When you've tested them, colour in the bowl.

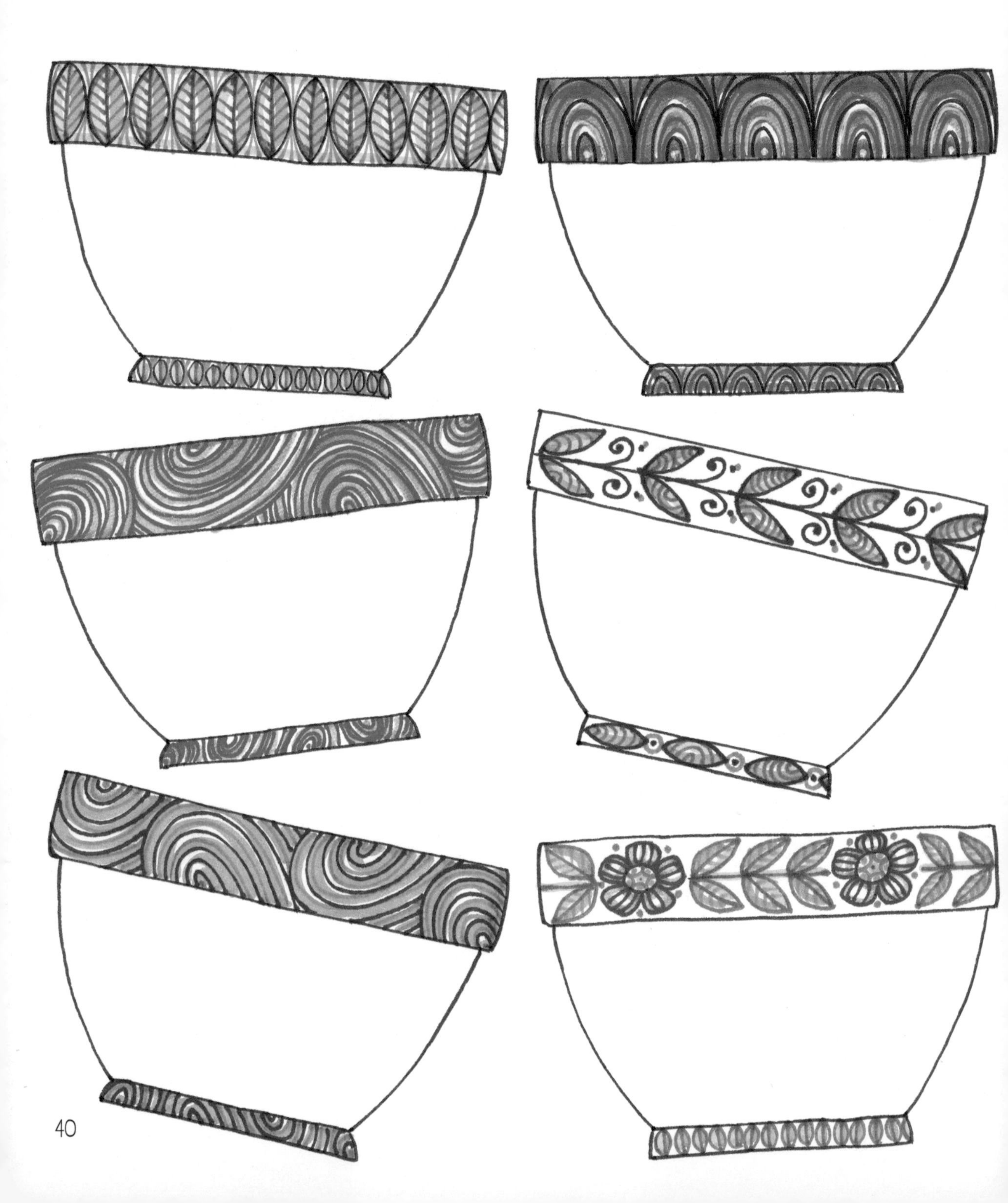

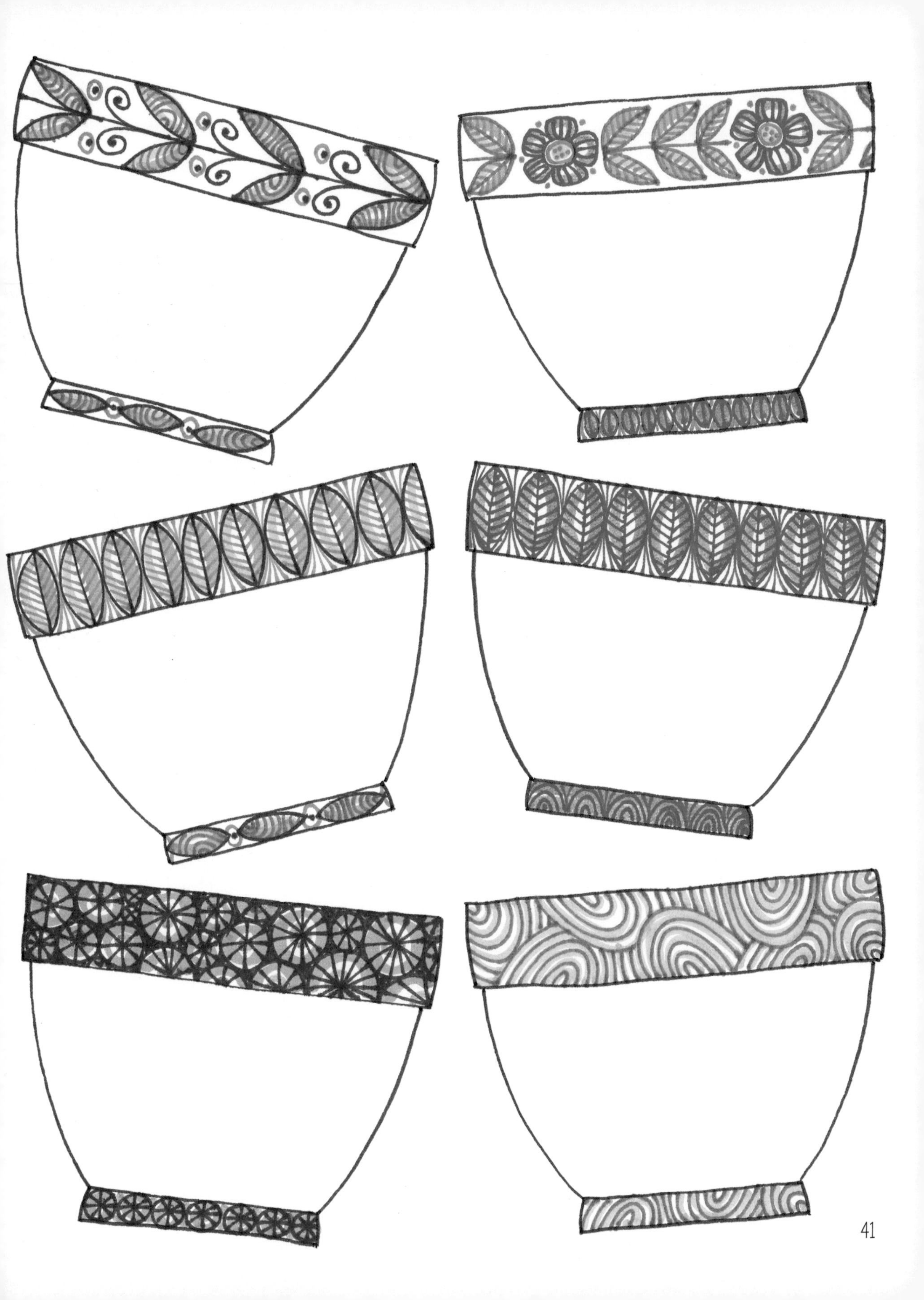

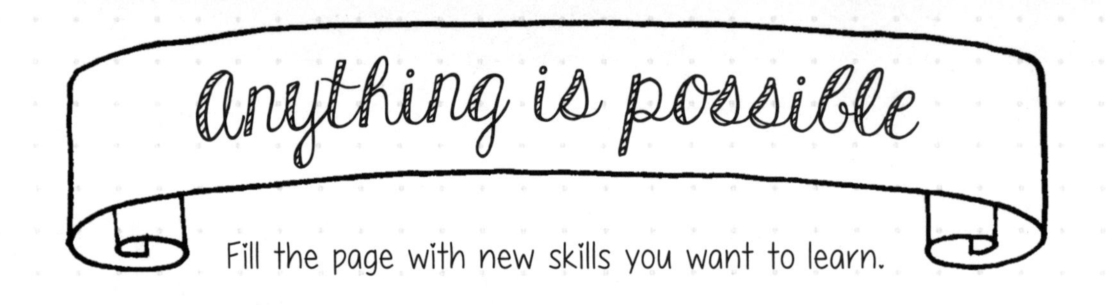

Fill the page with new skills you want to learn.

Favourites

Favourite quotes

Choose your favourite quotes and write them below.

Favourite songs

Record your favourite songs here.

Favourite things

Choose your favourite things and write them inside the pictures.

TV SHOW
DRINK
CELEBRITY
BAND
FOOD
BOOK

Favourite food

Complete the page with all your favourite foods and add doodles and pictures.

Favourite places

Choose your favourite places and write them below.

Favourite people

Jot down all your favourite
people and add decorative doodles
to the page if you want to.

Happy
and
healthy

Happy chart

On the left-hand side of the chart, write the things you do in your free time. Choose how often each activity makes you feel better and colour in the corresponding box on the chart. If you need a burst of good feelings, look at the chart and do the things that help the most.

Pocket full of sunshine

When someone does something to brighten your day, write it in a sun ray. Then pass it on by doing the same for someone else. Colour in the sun ray once you've done it. You could also fill it in with patterns.

Positive thoughts

Use each cloud below to write a positive thought that will inspire you when you need it most.

Self care

Fill in the columns with the things you do that make you feel good. You can look back at this page, add to it, and remind yourself what makes you feel your best.

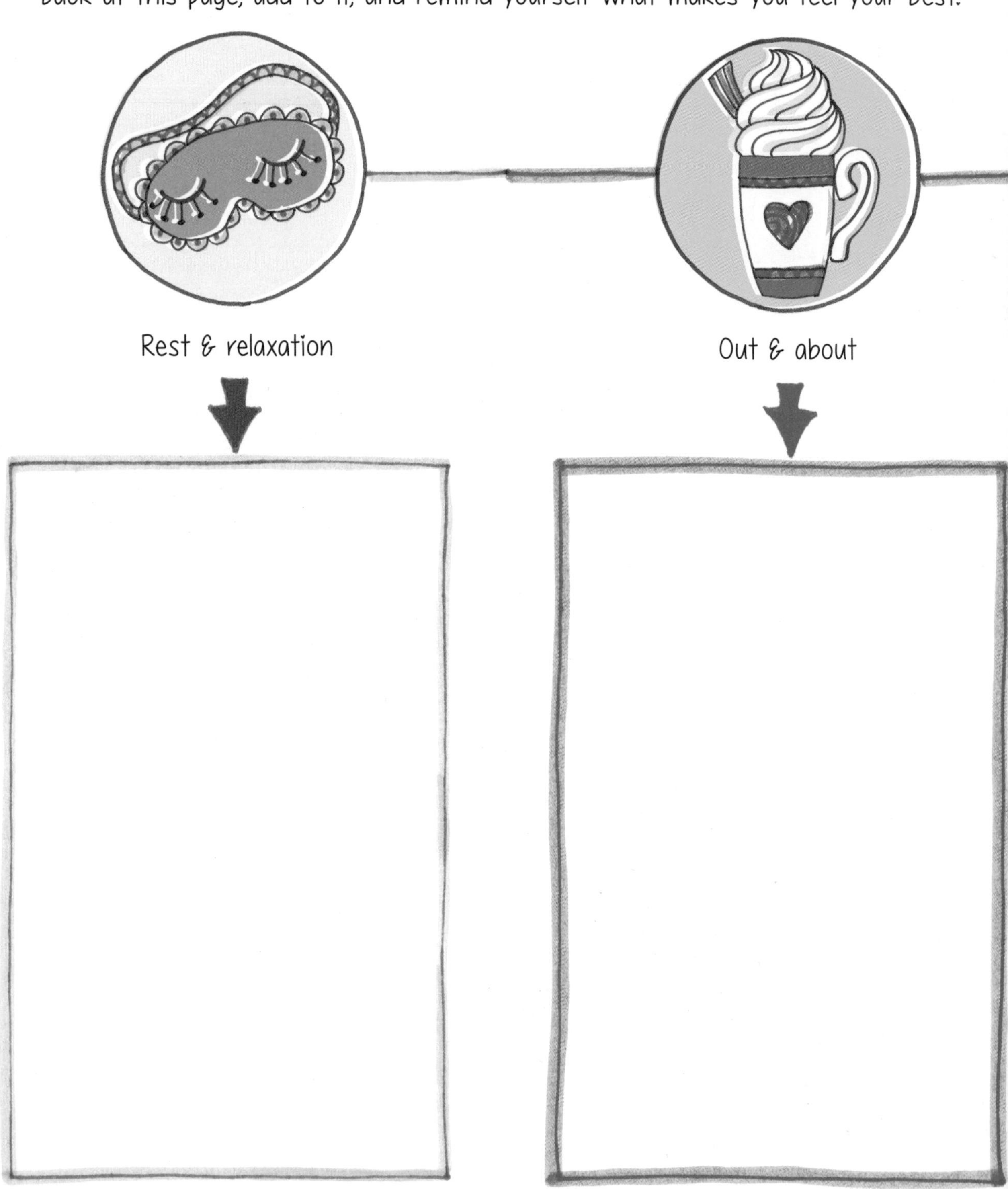

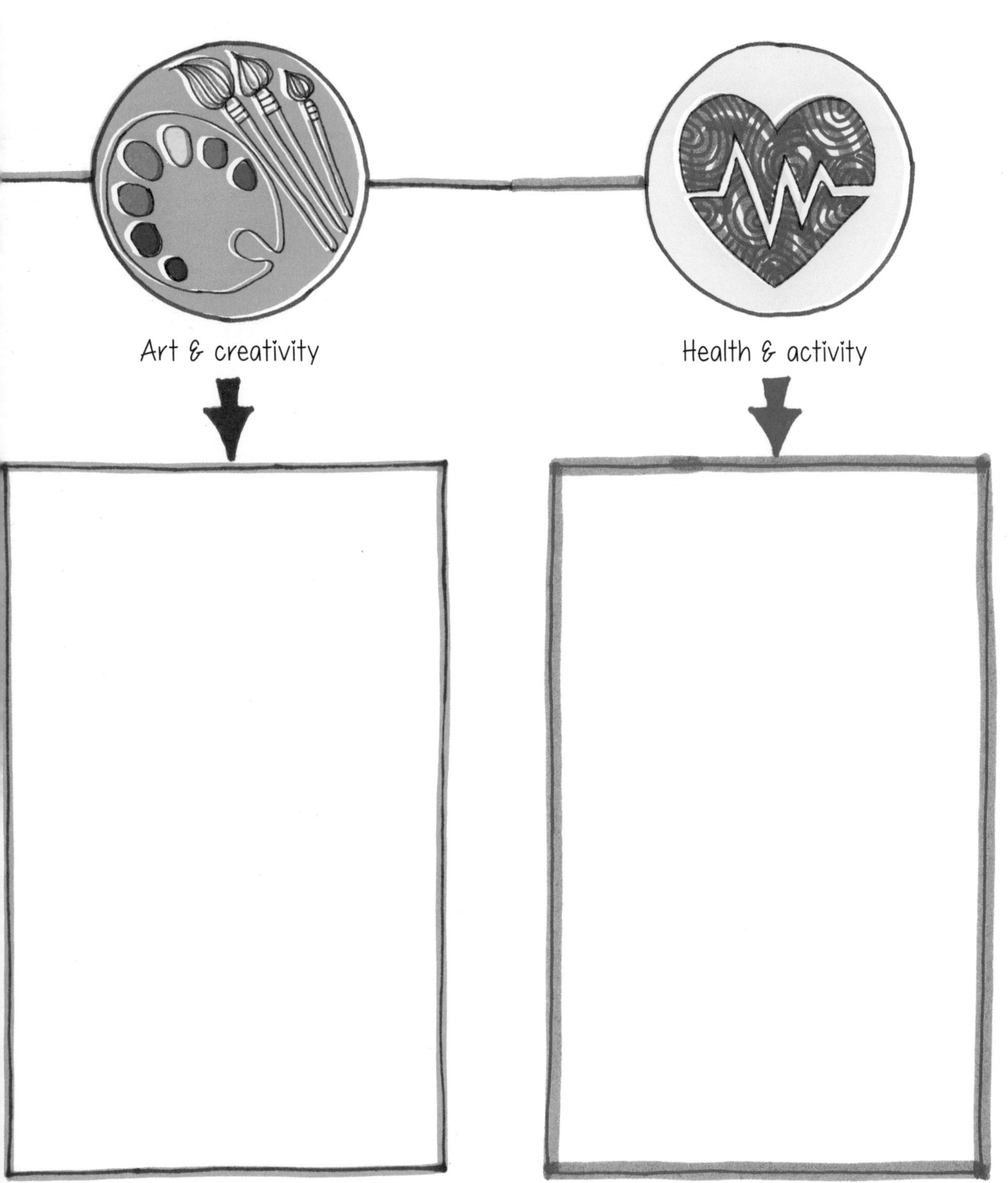
Art & creativity
Health & activity

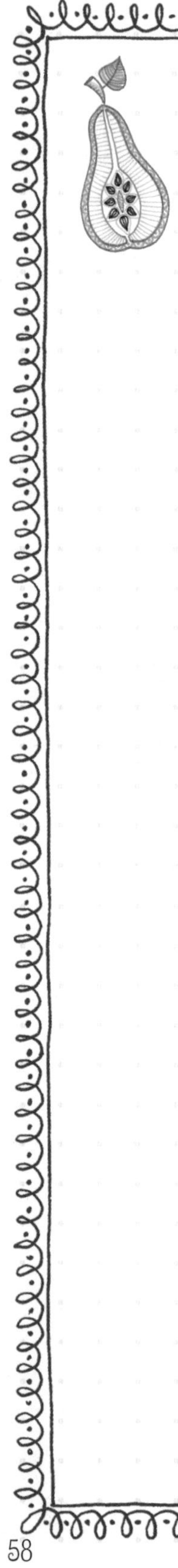

Healthy snacks

Jot down lots of ideas for healthy snacks. You can look back at this page when you're feeling hungry and don't know what to eat.

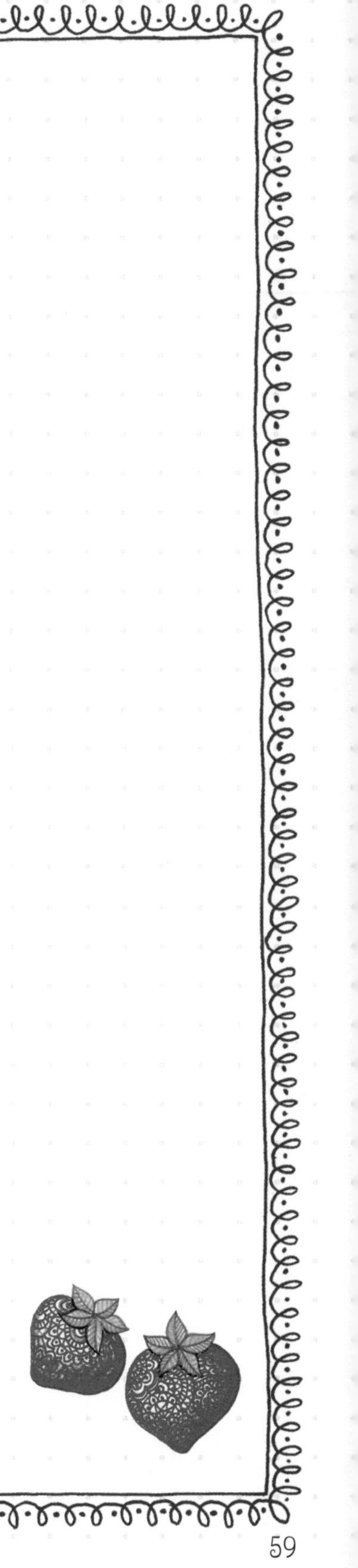

Compliment bouquet

Fill in each petal with compliments. Use the flower on this page to fill in nice things you have said to other people, and the flower on the next page to write down nice things people have said to you.

Change the world

Fill in each cloud with something you would do to make the world a better place.

Picture perfect

Draw and doodle all the things that
make you happy on this page.

Planned
to
perfection

Happy birthday
Keep track of your friends' and family's birthdays by writing them around the birthday wheels.
January
February
March
April
May
June

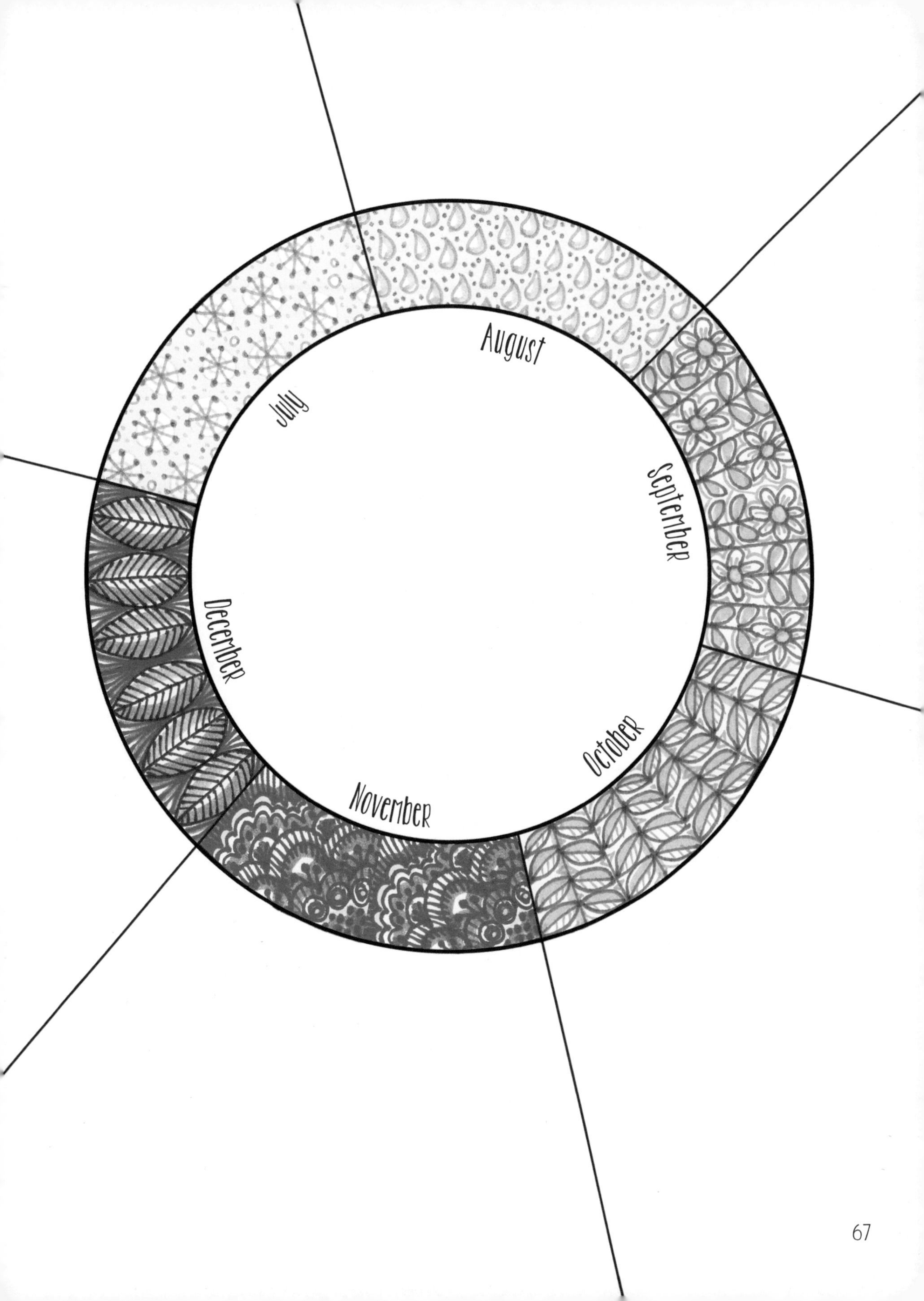
July
August
September
October
November
December

Wheel of life

Track your monthly activities by colouring in a segment in each section when you do it. You'll be able to see how much time you are dedicating to each aspect of your life.

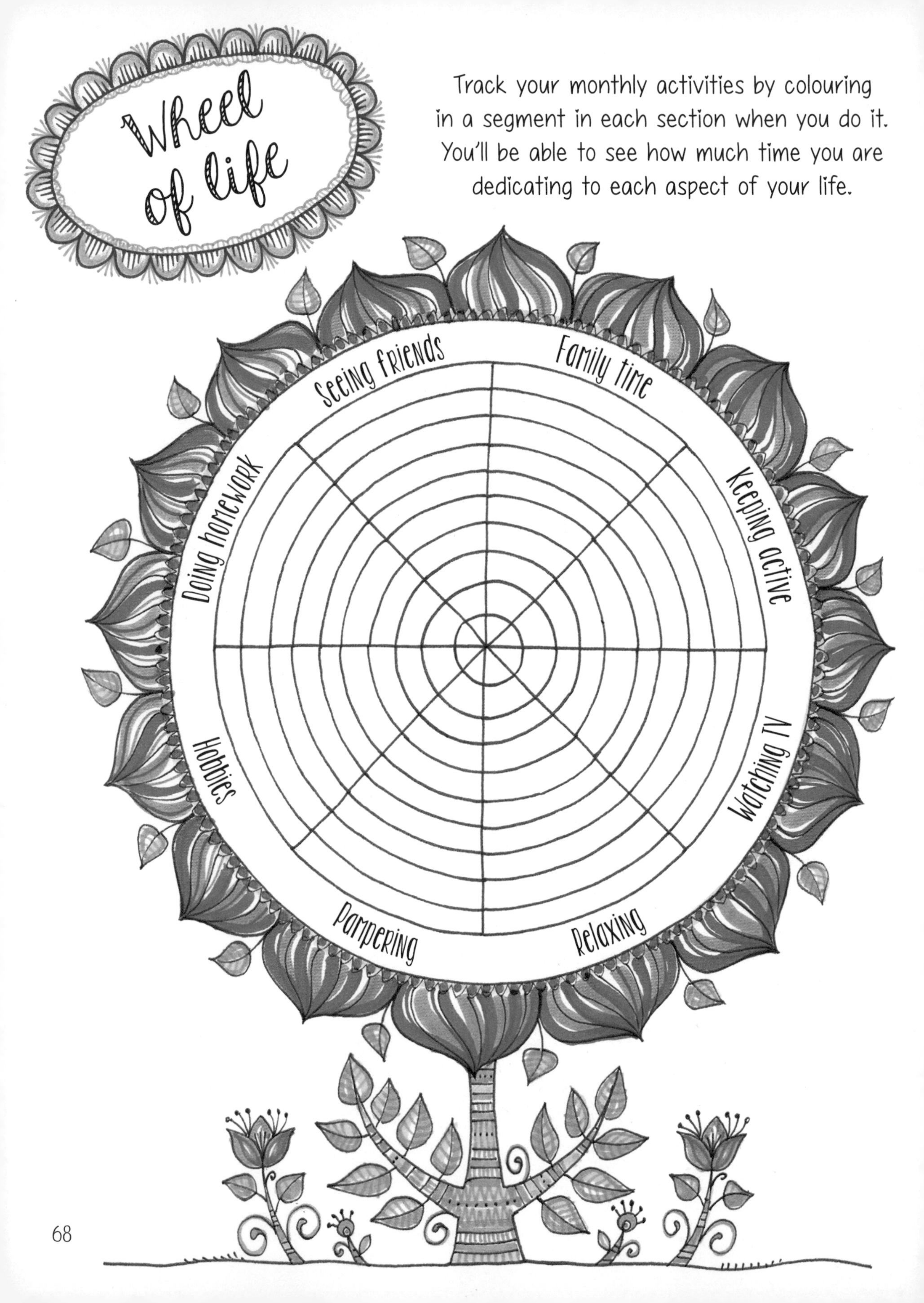

Saving goals

Colour in each section of the jar as you get closer to your goal and write how much you have saved beside it.

I am saving for ....

It costs ....

Every week/month I will save ....

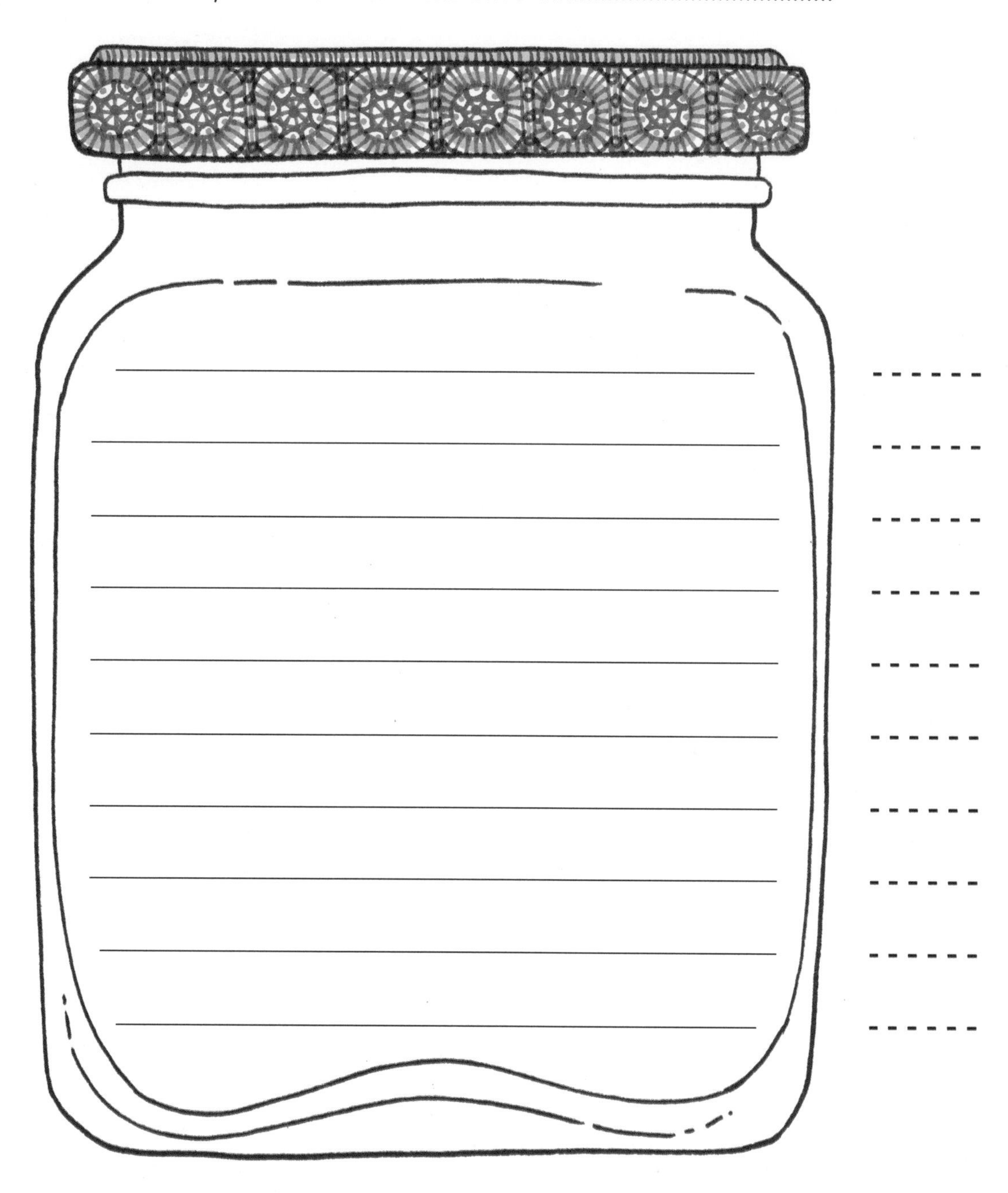

Present ideas

Fill in each gift box with an idea for a present to get a friend or family member. Look back at this page when gift-giving events are approaching.

Homework deadlines

Fill in your homework deadlines below, then colour in the book pages when you have completed the task.

Packing for holidays

Fill up the suitcase with a list of all the things you need to pack for your holidays so you don't forget any essential items.

Five-minute tasks

Scribble some quick tasks in the segments below. Colour in the segment when you've finished each task to show your progress.

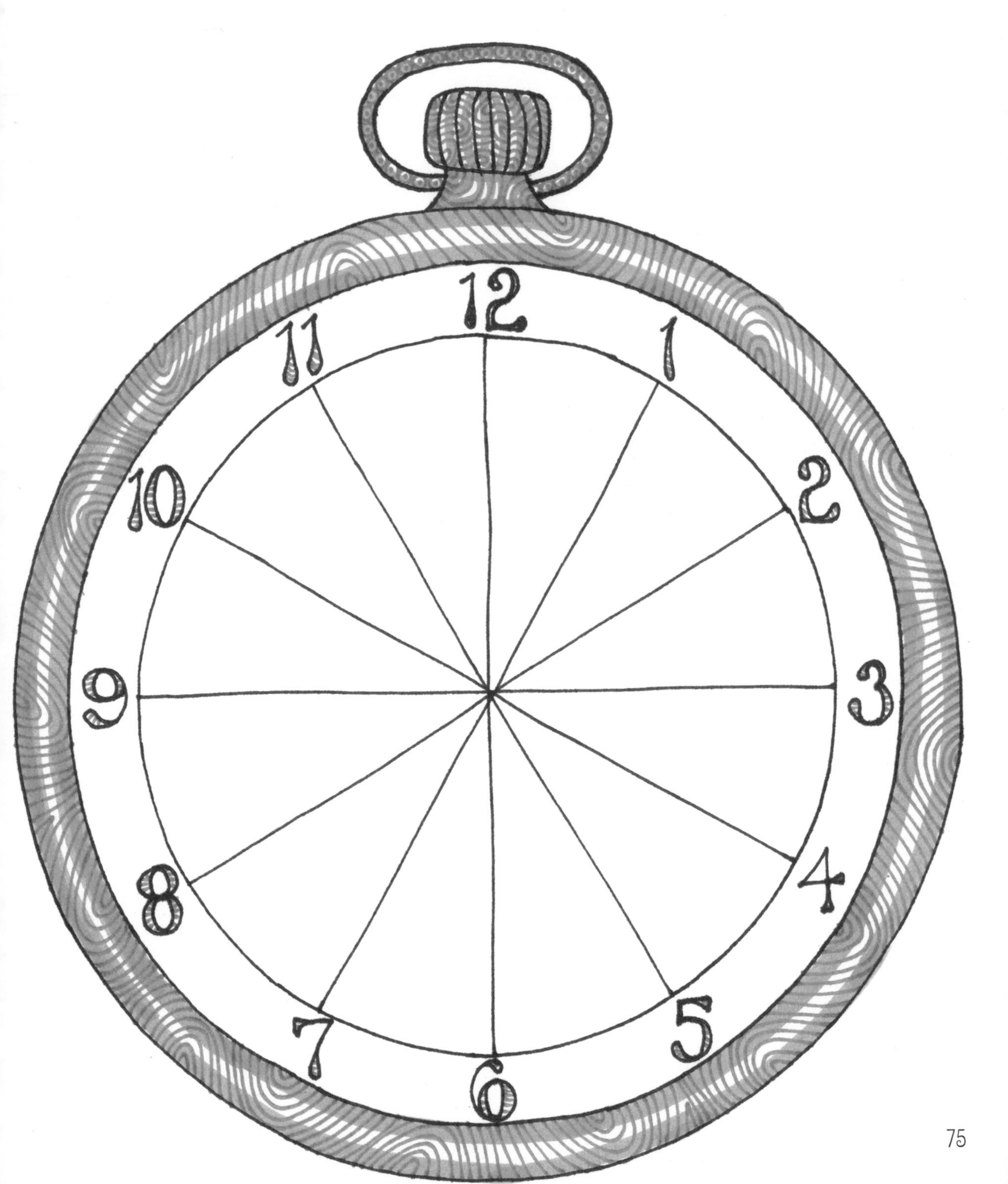

Weekend fun

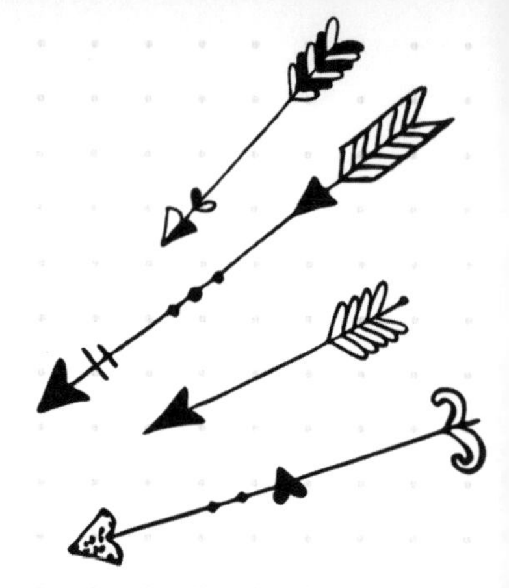

Jot down all of the things
you enjoy doing at the weekend.

Music
playlists

What are your all-time happy songs?

Jot down your favourite chill-out tunes.

Make a playlist of your
favourite energetic songs.

Write down the music you like
to listen to on a rainy day when you're stuck inside.

What are your ultimate
upbeat party songs?

Month by month

January

Jot down your plans for January so
you can keep track of all your tasks.

February

Jot down your plans for February so you can keep track of all your tasks.

March

Jot down your plans for March so
you can keep track of all your tasks.

April

Jot down your plans for April so
you can keep track of all your tasks.

May

Jot down your plans for May so you can keep track of all your tasks.

June

Jot down your plans for June so
you can keep track of all your tasks.

July

Jot down your plans for July so you can keep track of all your tasks.

August

Jot down your plans for August so you can keep track of all your tasks.

September

Jot down your plans for September so you can keep track of all your tasks.

October

Jot down your plans for October so you can keep track of all your tasks.

November

Jot down your plans for November so you can keep track of all your tasks.

December

Jot down your plans for December so
you can keep track of all your tasks.

Fill in different moods on the colour keys below. Then colour in each day of each month depending on how you were feeling.

February mood tracker
February
1st
2Nd
3Rd
4th
5th
6th
7th
8th
9th
10th
11th
12th
13th
14th
15th
16th
17th
18th
19th
20th
21st
22Nd
23Rd
24th
25th
26th
27th
28th
29th
Creative
Relaxed
Energized

March mood tracker
march
1st
2nd
3rd
4th
5th
6th
7th
8th
9th
10th
11th
12th
13th
14th
15th
16th
17th
18th
19th
20th
21st
22nd
23rd
24th
25th
26th
27th
28th
29th
30th
31st
Creative
Relaxed
Energized

April mood tracker
April
1st
2nd
3rd
4th
5th
6th
7th
8th
9th
10th
11th
12th
13th
14th
15th
16th
17th
18th
19th
20th
21st
22nd
23rd
24th
25th
26th
27th
28th
29th
30th
Creative
Relaxed
Energized

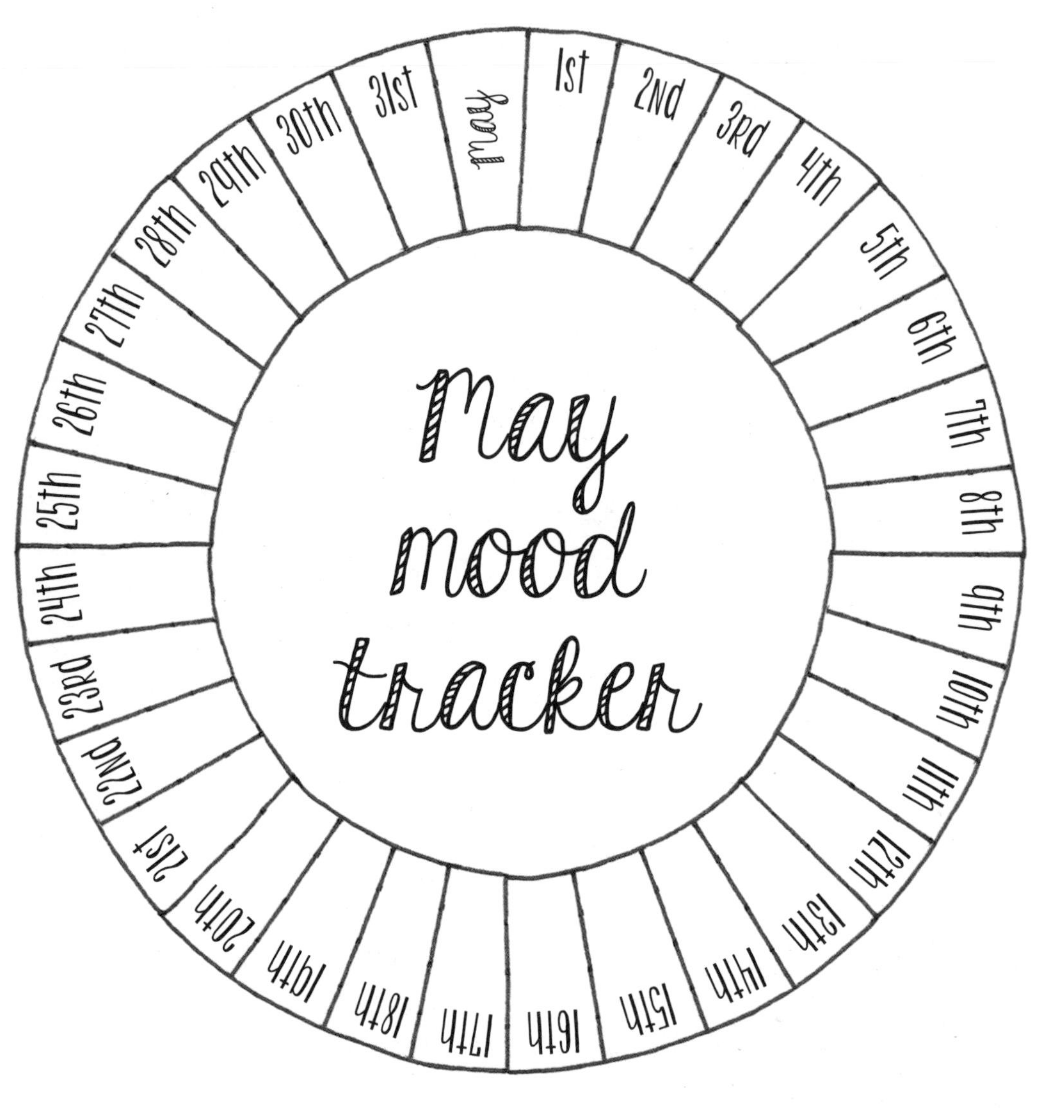

- Creative
- Relaxed
- Energized
- ....
- ....
- ....
- ....
- ....

June mood tracker
June
1st
2nd
3rd
4th
5th
6th
7th
8th
9th
10th
11th
12th
13th
14th
15th
16th
17th
18th
19th
20th
21st
22nd
23rd
24th
25th
26th
27th
28th
29th
30th
Creative
Relaxed
Energized

July
1st
2nd
3rd
4th
5th
6th
7th
8th
9th
10th
11th
12th
13th
14th
15th
16th
17th
18th
19th
20th
21st
22nd
23rd
24th
25th
26th
27th
28th
29th
30th
31st
July mood tracker
Creative
Relaxed
Energized

August mood tracker
August
1st
2Nd
3Rd
4th
5th
6th
7th
8th
9th
10th
11th
12th
13th
14th
15th
16th
17th
18th
19th
20th
21st
22Nd
23Rd
24th
25th
26th
27th
28th
29th
30th
31st
Creative
Relaxed
Energized

September mood tracker
September
1st
2nd
3rd
4th
5th
6th
7th
8th
9th
10th
11th
12th
13th
14th
15th
16th
17th
18th
19th
20th
21st
22nd
23rd
24th
25th
26th
27th
28th
29th
30th
Creative
Relaxed
Energized

October mood tracker
October
1st
2nd
3rd
4th
5th
6th
7th
8th
9th
10th
11th
12th
13th
14th
15th
16th
17th
18th
19th
20th
21st
22nd
23rd
24th
25th
26th
27th
28th
29th
30th
31st
Creative
Relaxed
Energized

November mood tracker
November
1st
2nd
3rd
4th
5th
6th
7th
8th
9th
10th
11th
12th
13th
14th
15th
16th
17th
18th
19th
20th
21st
22nd
23rd
24th
25th
26th
27th
28th
29th
30th
Creative
Relaxed
Energized

December
1st
2nd
3rd
4th
5th
6th
7th
8th
9th
10th
11th
12th
13th
14th
15th
16th
17th
18th
19th
20th
21st
22nd
23rd
24th
25th
26th
27th
28th
29th
30th
31st
December mood tracker
Creative
Relaxed
Energized

Habit tracker

Label the colour key with your activities and then colour in each day of the month using your key. You can track what you have been doing over the year.

Checklists

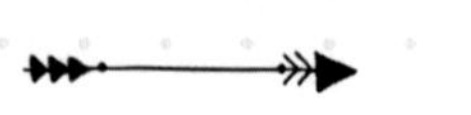

Checklist